THAT ALL MEN BE ONE

To my very dear
    Sisters in Carmel —

That we all may be
one in His love
        Fondly,
        Emma G.

THAT ALL MEN BE ONE

*Origins and Life of
the Focolare Movement*

by
Chiara Lubich

New City Press
London - New York - Hong Kong - Manila - Melbourne

Published in the United States by New City Press.
© by Citta Nuova Editrice. Printed in Hong Kong.

Second Printing, 1973

Nihil obstat: Martinus S. Rushford, Ph. D.
Censor Librorum

Imprimatur: † Franciscus Ioannes Mugavero, D. D.
Episcopus Bruklyniensis
Bruklyni die iv februarii 1969

Library of Congress Catalog Card Number: 71-77438

This book is dedicated
to the increasing numbers of people interested
in knowing of the events and ideas
that contributed to the birth and growth
of the Focolare Movement.
It is a brief account
of an extraordinary story
that had as its protagonists,
young people with a strong belief in God's love,
and a loving God.
This human-divine dialogue,
which has as its principal setting,
the Second World War,
is recounted by
one of its central participants,
Chiara Lubich,
whom we thank
for providing us with this material,
of such great interest and relevance,
for so many people.

Contents

Contents

I

Milestones along Our Way

IT SEEMS TO BE A CHARACTERISTIC of the things of God that they begin on the scale of the mustard seed. Some twenty-five years ago in Trent, there was only a small group of us. We were just girls, children, you might say. The youngest was fifteen. But as we know, young people are quick to have dreams and ideals. I lived for philosophy. My companion looked ahead to a nice family. Another longed to have a lovely, well-built home.

It was wartime. Bombs were destroying parts of the city and leaving their victims. These very bombs became the means whereby the Lord spoke his sermon, to us too, merely girls at the time. Since everything around us was being shattered, our ideals met the same fate. I could no longer continue my philosophy courses. They

were given in a city impossible to reach because
of the war. My friend's fiancé never returned
from battle. The others too saw their dreams
blown away. Houses, schools, works of art, all
the things they had set their hearts upon, were
destroyed. The lesson our Lord was teaching
could be summed up in one sentence: " All is
vanity of vanities and all things pass away. "

Faced by this spectacle, this pile of ruins and
rubble, we asked ourselves if there was any ideal
that would not pass, any ideal that no bomb
could shatter. And as by some inner illumination,
we immediately saw the answer. There is such an
ideal. God. God is everlasting.

By some supernatural force, we were driven
to choose, as the ideal of our lives, God.

We were very young, yet at any moment we
could have lost our lives. The shelters we fled
to were not safe from the bombs. This made
sharp in our minds, the ever present possibility
of our having to go before God. It was a constant
source of meditation, increasing in us the desire
to find the way in which God would become
truly, and as quickly as possible, our ideal.

Whenever we went into the shelters (up to
twelve times a day), we took with us the Gospel.
One day we came across the words, " Not every
one who says to me, ' Lord, Lord,' shall enter the

kingdom of heaven, but he who does the will of my Father who is in heaven. " This was our answer. If we wanted God as our ideal, we had to do his will. Loving God was not basically a matter of feelings, but one of the will. We tried to do his divine will, made clear by circumstances, by the duties of our calling in life, by those who were in authority over us, by our inspirations. We tried, moment by moment, each present moment that was given to us. The past was already past, and the future, even what was then the near future, could have found us already in the other life.

Never going outside of God's will—this was how we could show concretely that we loved him.

There was something else we wondered about at the time. Was there some will of God for us that was especially pleasing to Jesus, one that would have made him happy with us if we should have at once had to go before him?

Again the Gospel had the answer. " A new commandment I give to you, that you love one another; even as I have loved you, that you also love one another." We began to see each other in a new way; we decided to be, in our little group, the concrete expression of this commandment Jesus had called " his."

Jesus had loved us to the point of dying for

us. We had to be ready to die for one another. This worked in us something of a conversion. We decided in our hearts to put at the base of our lives, whatever direction they took, mutual and constant charity.

We asked ourselves, even before going to Mass and Communion in the morning, if we were ready to die for one another. The Gospel had said, " If you are offering your gift at the altar and there remember that your brother has something against you, leave your gift there before the altar and go; first be reconciled to your brother, and then come and offer your gift. "

Charity was to come before everything, before going to school or to the office, before going to sleep at night.

It wasn't that the Lord would necessarily ask us to die for one another; this was the extreme test of love. He asked of us, other, smaller things. If, for example, one of us was suffering, all would suffer with her, and the cross would be portioned out among us. If she was filled with great joy, we would all participate in it, thereby multiplying the joy. Or, as I recall, one of us had two coats while another had none. Naturally, the one with gave to the one without. If I had a good idea, one that helped me to love the Lord more, I shared it. My companions did the same.

Love led us to share what we had, our material goods and our spiritual goods.

We went continuously through this exercise of loving one another as Jesus had loved us.

The results? First, we experienced within, the fruits of the spirit, of which St. Paul spoke: the fullness of joy, of light, of peace.

Scripture says that where there is charity and love there is God. By practicing among ourselves mutual and constant charity, we had God to help us understand better the words of revelation. I mentioned that we brought with us into the shelters, the Gospels. It was as if there, we were reading them for the first time. God himself seemed to be explaining them to us.

These words seemed to us to be unique. All other writings, those of spiritual books too, appeared watered down by comparison. These were *words of life*; they could be translated at once into life. " Love your neighbor as yourself. " This could be practiced at any time; there is always a neighbor close by. " As you did it to one of the least of these my brethren, you did it to me. " This too could be lived at once. What's more, they were words for everybody, of universal application. The words of God were light, showered upon the earth for all; they were words that anyone, great or small, gifted or limited, could live.

Within us and around us, these words set off a revolution.

I must admit that until that time, I had not really taken seriously enough the word of God, even though I was a practicing Catholic. The Gospel had not been the law of my life. Now, by living the Gospel, the relationship that I and my companions had with God and with those around us, changed.

The Gospel always made clear how we were to conduct ourselves, even with our enemies: " Love your enemies, do good to those who hate you. "

Living these things, it was natural for people around us to ask why we loved everyone or what it was that made us act the way we did. Our response was simply this: " Come home with us and we'll tell you about it." When they did, we would tell of our discovery of an ideal that will not die. People understood; the lesson of the war was theirs to see. Around our little group, there began to grow a community of persons who wanted to live this ideal.

Within a few months, there were 500 of us in the city of Trent who were living the Gospel, which by its very nature was a bond of unity among us.

The whole of the Gospels became object for meditation and the law of the new life we had set out upon.

From the very beginning, certain passages stood out in a particular way, especially those that spoke explicitly of the love of God and neighbor and of unity.

One passage made a deep impression: " Father, that they may all be one. " This led us at once to love everybody without the least distinction, and to put ourselves at God's disposal for the realization of this, his will and testament.

Another phrase struck home deeply: " Where two or three are gathered in my name, there am I in the midst of them. " The joy of being united as brothers in Christ was a discovery we did not want to lose. We wanted Christ always to be in our midst.

His mystical presence had these effects: it enabled us to have unity, it enabled us to begin realizing the words of Jesus in the Gospel, " That they may all be one ... that the world may believe. "

We went ahead in this way, driven forward by the grace of God. One day, however, we read in the Gospel these words: " Who listens to you listens to me. " This gave us to understand that the one who could tell us if we were on the right road or not would be the bishop. We went to him and told him of all that we were doing. " Here we have the hand of God, " were his words, and he encouraged us to go ahead, never to stop.

The Movement spread widely and rapidly. We credit its extension on a broad international scale to our close-knit, newfound unity with the hierarchy, by which we are more deeply rooted in Christ, whom it represents. We attribute this expansion to the unity we have among ourselves. Jesus in our midst witnesses the truth to the world and the world is being won over by him.

We have reached out to every part of Italy. There is hardly a city on the peninsula where the Movement has not struck roots.

Since 1958, we have spread to other European countries, to Germany, to France, to Belgium, to Holland, to Spain, to England, and so on.

Today, we are also in Brazil, Argentina, the United States, Canada, the Philippines, Japan, Australia, Africa.

This I recount only to glorify God. No human force could ever have accomplished such a thing.

The chief effects of God's work through this Movement are conversions. Men change over to

16

God. How many are the non-believers who have gone over to him! They have been moved by the testimony of unity coming from people of diverse nations and races who are one in the name of Christ; by the testimony of persons representing the most diverse social categories, who are united in the name of Christ, just as were the first Christian communities.

Sinners and atheists have gone over to God. Listless souls, people who thought themselves good, have become ardent proponents of the love of Christ and neighbor.

Christ in our midst has given rise to vocations. How numerous are the young men who have turned to the priesthood and are now solidly united with their bishops!

Why have countless religious orders found a source of renewal in this spirit? Because this spirit is charity; it is love, as understood in the New Testament: " God is love."

When this love takes hold in a monastery or a religious house, there enters in his fullness, God, and he works a change. Those living there become more united with God, with their superiors. Greater unity is built among the various religious orders.

A further outcome of Christ's presence is this: God steps into the world of the layman. Lay persons steeped in this spirit become in fact, what the Vatican Council desires and foresees in their regard. The Council has stated that the whole Church has to be apostolic, to be missionary. This includes the laity. The whole Church is to incline toward sanctity. This includes the laity. We know that sanctity lies in charity, through which God can enter the factory, the school, government, the family. Many are the families in which father, mother, and children are living in unity, in the spirit of the Good News. They share their experiences to help one another advance in God's love. They live in the midst of the world, and there, help to transform the social fabric of their surroundings.

Something of what Pius XII called. " the consecration of the world " is coming about through this spirit.

The laity is awakening; it feels itself " Church, " and wants to work together with those in responsible positions for the glory of God, toward the renewal and the building up of the Church.

There we have some main lines of the Movement. But we might ask what there is new in them. Nothing really new. New is the resolve to live the Gospel, today, along these lines. New is the synthesis of the realities that stand out in the Movement—mutual love, Jesus in our midst, living as Mystical Body, a sense of the Church, unity. These are truths that have always been in the Gospels, but perhaps God is putting them in a greater light in these times. It is enough to think of how much the entire Christian world is talking of love, of communion and of the community.

Until 1960 we thought of the Movement as coming from God solely for the Roman Catholic Church. We were Catholics and knew little about Christians of other denominations. No one of us connected the Movement with ecumenism. (The plans for this Movement are in God, not in men.) But in 1960, we met with some Lutherans. We told them of our experiences. Above all, we showed our love for them. They displayed much interest. At first we were in contact with their *Brudershaften vom Gemeinsamen Leben* (" brotherhood of the common life "). Then, some ministers asked that we talk to them and become acquainted with their congregations. Theologians ' called upon us to speak to other theologians. Meanwhile, some Evangelicals asked to know better the Catholic Church, especially in Italy. We spent time together with them at Assisi, at Florence, at Trent, at

19

Rome, at Naples, and many other places, always in a wonderful spirit of mutual charity.

For them too, this life we had set out upon was like a rediscovery of the Gospel. They set themselves to living it, to introducing this spirit into their congregations and associations. This activity, this communion has been continuing now for a good number of years. Thousands are the Lutherans we now know and love as our brothers in Christ. They are brothers not only through our common baptism, but also through our common effort to re-model our lives in the spirit of the Gospel, and especially in the spirit of mutual love.

We want to have together with them, Jesus in our midst. If we are baptized, Jesus can be in the midst of us. And one thing is certain; the greatest theologian is Jesus. If he is in our midst, he is there not only as love, but as truth. Should we work to have him always among us, looking first, as Pope John said, to what unites us, it will eventually be Jesus in our midst to unravel the truth and reconcile those theological divergencies that yet keep us apart.

It is well known how the Evangelical Lutherans have their difficulties with the Catholic Church. But in the case of those we know, many, many difficulties are fading away. Each time our

Lutheran friends come to Rome, for example, they seek an audience with the Pope. They've understood that he too is to be loved. They've shown a desire also to know our bishops and our religious orders.

On our part, we have come to know and value the great love the Evangelicals have for the word of God and their deep spirit of prayer.

Knowing one another gives birth to love; we become aware that we are brothers; we find how much is common to all of us.

We were twice received in audience by the Lutheran bishop of Bavaria, Dr. Dietzfelbinger, who has since been elected President of the German Lutherans. He is much taken by our spirituality and has always given his support to our ecumenical work.

A time came when we saw the necessity of placing these contacts between Catholics and Lutherans on an uninterrupted basis. With the permission of our respective superiors, and with the blessing of our bishop, the Most Rev. Joseph Stimpfle, and theirs, the same Dr Dietzfelbinger, a center was set up at Augsburg, Germany. There, Catholics and Lutherans, living together, can, on an extended basis, know and love and appreciate one another better.

During one of our gatherings a few years

back with the Lutherans at Rocca di Papa near Rome, some Anglican priests were present. They were deeply impressed by this family-like reunion. From that time on we have been very close with them. This has been of immense benefit. There were so many things about the Church of England we formerly did not know but now value highly. And they too have found out many things about the Catholic Church.

The Archbishop of Canterbury himself, Dr. Ramsey, saw fit to invite us to visit him in London. After we explained something of the Movement, he said to us, " I am filled with gratitude for the hand of God in this work. You have much to offer to the Church of England. There are many ways in which you can work in contact with the Anglicans and have a spiritual communion with them in this country, such that their hearts can be warmed by the fire of this spirit. "

In North and South America, too, we have had of recent years, innumerable contacts with other denominations.

Though once solely in the Catholic Church, the Movement is now striking roots in a large sector of Christianity. Great numbers are seeking to live its spirit within their possibilities, according to their understanding of it.

Some years ago we were in the Holy Land. There we saw diverse Christian denominations disputing over possession of the holy places. The sight of Jesus' tomb filled us with sorrow. It too was divided. It belonged to three different Christian denominations. Jerusalem seemed to be the city of Christians disunited.

Yet it was there, before that tomb, that we found new hope. Why was it that they fought to have a piece of Jesus' tomb? It was because they loved Jesus. Each faction loved Jesus in its own way. This made us see something. The day in which all Christians will come to understand that to love God means to do his will, and that his will is above all for men to love one another, then no longer will there be disputes. Rather, there will be mutual love and the whole tomb will belong to everybody. And so too the Church.

Many are the times when our non-Catholic Christian brothers come to visit Rome and the Catacombs, the Colosseum with its memories of the martyrs, the Basilica of St. Paul and of St. Peter, and all the beauties of the Eternal City. Each time they come we feel we would like to tell them that all this is theirs too; it belongs to all of us because here, in these places, our forefathers were united.

And when we go to Germany, for example, and see those magnificent Gothic churches of the Lutherans, we spontaneously find ourselves asking our friends what is stopping us from having a communion of goods among us, with all the wonderful advantages it would work for everybody.

This, unfortunately, has not yet come about!

Not long ago, however, some Anglicans and Lutherans came to visit a little ecumenical town of ours, Loppiano, near Florence, where Christianity is a fact, where everybody loves one another and Jesus reigns in the midst of all. Together, we came to a conclusion: We all feel at home in this spirituality; we all seek to live the Gospel. Our ecclesiastical authority has approved the Movement. Non-Catholic Christians too can be a part of it. So then, everything that is ours in the Movement belongs not only to us Catholics but also to the Anglicans, to the Lutherans, and to all those who live this spirit. Our centers are theirs too, then! our little towns, our publishing activities. Likewise the Lutherans and Anglicans present, knowing their ecclesiastical authorities had expressed satisfaction and the desire that this spirit penetrate their Churches, said in turn that what was theirs was ours too.

From these things came more new hope. What

is impossible with men is possible with God. If we, of such diverse denominations, have God in our midst, for him everything will be possible. We feel deeply the words of an Anglican bishop present for a gathering of the Movement one Easter in Rome. He said that the more we know one another, the more the division will become unbearable.

Then there is the most recent encounter we have had in the brief history of our Movement.

We have had contacts on an individual basis with various Orthodox personalities, but our real meeting with that Church came about on June 13, 1966 when we met with Patriarch Athenagoras.

The Patriarch now knows the Movement and wants the spread of its spirit.

There are now at Istanbul deep feelings of love and respect between Christians of the Orthodox and Catholic Churches.

II

The World Was Not So Dark

A T THE BEGINNING of the Movement, we encountered a great reality. God. This reality alone gave meaning to the whole of the Movement's subsequent life and growth.

God, the most blessed Trinity, shone out like the sun at the dawn of a world that was once more rediscovering the ways of peace after the strident noises of war, offering to us, his children, a more divine way of life than the good lives which some of us were already leading; more Christianly coherent, more integral.

Other young women had separately, at other times and in quite different circumstances, felt called to live this very same ideal.

And together, in the Franciscan atmosphere in which the Movement grew, we often thought of St. Clare.

" My child, what is it you desire? " St. Francis had asked when, at eighteen, she fled from home to follow the Lord.

" God," she had replied.

God! For us too, under the impulse of grace, this reality alone, unique, infinite, contained the sum total of our aspirations. We felt an ardent desire to remain faithful to Him, as the saints had done, for as long as we lived.

God alone, and nothing else, since any other person or thing would have detracted from the beauty of the divine call.

From the very first instant, God, for us, was synonymous with Love.

It is thus that Holy Scripture speaks of Him: " God is Love. "

This God, who is Love, was our All.

This was a great discovery in our spiritual lives, so great that it affected a kind of conversion.

Previously, while trying to be good, practicing Christians, to live in God's grace, we had really been like orphans, like people that had a father and mother, but only upon this earth. But later, with this new realization of God as love, we were more fully conscious of being children of our Father in heaven. We felt, in a way, like St. Francis when he addressed his own father: " No

longer do I say ' Father Bernardone', but ' our
Father who art in heaven.' "

There was a closer link now between heaven
and earth, a new understanding between the
children and their Father.

It seemed as if a new faith had matured in us,
no longer merely a faith in God, which we
already possessed, but a faith in his love. We
felt no words were more applicable to the life
we had set out upon than the phrase from the
Bible, " We believe the love God has for us. "

From then on, the whole of our lives were lit
up by this faith in the love of God for us, for
each one and for all, for the whole of humanity.

God loved us! He was our Creator, the one
who sustained us moment by moment. He was
our All! Our lives on this earth would be
meaningless unless we became like little sparks
of this infinite flame, our love responding to
Love.

So sublime was this dignity to which he had
elevated us, so lofty and unmerited this possibility
of loving him, that we repeatedly reminded
ourselves: " We must not say we are obliged to
love God, but rather: ' Oh, to be able to love
you Lord! to love you with this small heart of
ours! ' "

We tried hard to do this.

As the days, weeks and years passed, it became clear to us that He would not let himself be outdone in generosity.

Holy Scripture says that He will manifest himself to the person who loves him (John 14, 21), and this, perhaps, was why, step by step, he revealed to us the treasures that he himself had prepared for us on earth: the different forms of his presence, diverse but ever the same, in this place of exile, where we live in expectation of heaven. This presence led us to see ever more clearly how infinite is his love, how unlimitedly resourceful are the ways of his fatherly love for us. He led us to where we might find him, that we might resemble him more closely; he showed us how we might possess him. In brief, he indicated to us how, and by what means, the union of our souls with him might come to birth and mature.

He did not take us to a hermitage, or to a cloistered convent, but to where the Prince of this world most completely holds sway, where the darkness is thickest: " Father, I am not asking you to remove them from the world, but to protect them from the evil one."

Like new-born children opening their eyes to the light for the first time, we realized that the coming of God on earth out of love had left the

world radically changed: He had remained on
earth with us.

In our travels, as we moved from place to
place, we were not drawn by the things and
events, however interesting and beautiful, that
each city or nation had to offer. Rome itself,
for example, was not primarily important to us
because of the wonderful historical monuments
and precious relics that it possesses. The links
in the chain of our far-flung travels for His sake
were, rather, Jesus himself in the tabernacles that
we passed.

Every church we sighted from a train window
was " home " for our souls.

When we visited some shrine, or the places
where our Saviour was born and died—places
where we would willingly have lingered
indefinitely—it was Jesus in the Eucharist who
gave us strength to depart and continue on our
way. For he is present in every corner of the
world; equally present in a small, remote Alpine
chapel, and in a majestic cathedral in some great
metropolis. Jesus in the Eucharist is like a light,
lit here and there by his own love, to comfort
young and old, rich and poor, educated and
uneducated. He is the universal Brother, the
same for all, who dries every tear, renews the

strength of every heart, and offers his spirit to those who live according to his law.

The world was not, then, so dark. Jesus in the Eucharist transformed it into a vast cloister, offering himself to satisfy the hunger for the divine that is liable to make itself felt in every soul.

Moreover, every neighbor, a schoolmate, a beggar, a man at the newsstand, a member of parliament, a child, an invalid, all appeared different to us now under the action of grace. In every neighbor we learned to recognize, and to love, a member of the Mystical Body, to see Christ.

As a result, those who might previously have been, for us, an obstacle in our ascent to God, now became a door that led to Him.

Holy Scripture had promised it: " We have passed out of death into life, because we love our brethren. "

The more we loved Christ in every person with complete forgetfulness of self, the more God filled our hearts, and the more surely the Lord made his soothing presence felt in our souls during our evening prayers.

This experience helped us to understand how pleasing to God is charity, and that the finest flower of the Gospel is brotherly love.

In certain people, who were our brothers also, we were not only to love God but also to obey him. They were God's representatives for us, our ecclesiastical superiors, our bishops and assistants; persons placed there with loving care by the Church.

They were the shepherds, we the sheep.

This effort to conduct ourselves, consciously, as children of God in the Church, the Spouse of Christ, like branches united to the vine, gradually had this effect on our souls: in time the Church itself seemed to live and throb in our hearts. We spontaneously identified our feelings *with the Church*, sharing in her struggles and victories, even to the point of desiring to shed our blood, with the help of God's grace, to ensure her triumph.

And then, the discovery of God in our midst.

At the beginning, when we tried to live the words of Jesus: "Where two or three are gathered in my name, there I am in the midst of them," it seemed that heaven itself enveloped us, that our souls were immersed in paradise. Jesus was again, spiritually, among us, brothers in him, and in a manner that recalled Emmaus. He lit in our hearts a flame that this world does not know, making our view of men and things fall back into the shade, and setting in relief

33

everything that is significant, beautiful and good before God.

Jesus present among Christians was like a temple resting on firm pillars—the hearts of his children united together—that could be set up in any locality, providing the consolation of a spiritual tabernacle, whether in a noisy street, in pagan lands or in the prison cells of those suffering unjustly for their convictions.

Jesus is always life and fullness, joy and paradise, guide and master. Our reciprocal love could be the powerful means whereby to render him present. We used to say: " If you cross a few logs together on the summit of a mountain, and then set a light to them, the flames will be seen throughout the length and breadth of the valley, shining as brightly as a star fallen on earth. But if we dispose, ' cross together, ' our hearts in a similar way, and love each other as He has loved us, we shall have *the* fire, Love itself, among us, and we shall be God's instruments in drawing many souls to him. "

God, then, was to be found in the Eucharist, loved in our neighbor, obeyed in our superiors. He was also spiritually present among us.

In our finite hearts, too, the infinite God is present, through grace. We were being called to help him reign there in his majesty, to demolish our own ego so as to be transformed in him.

God could also be found in the Scriptures. There he could be grasped and meditated on under the action of the Spirit and the guidance of the Church. From the endless riches of Scripture, those who desired to love him have drawn in the past, and will continue to do so until the end of the world. The blessed Virgin also pondered on the Scriptures, and we desired to imitate her who, like us, dwelt in the midst of men, for we wished to learn to give God to others, to the whole world.

To find God, in all places and at all times, God who is Love, who fills up the emptiness left by sin, the emptiness already amply made up for by the blood of Jesus—this is the goal and end of our lives.

III

Moment by Moment in a Ray of Sun

G OD . . . THE LOVE OF GOD.
But how does one go about loving him?
" Not everyone who says to me, ' Lord, Lord,'
shall enter the kingdom of heaven, but he who
does the will of my Father."

Loving him, then, was not mainly a matter of
feeling, but one of the will. It meant doing his
will.

A simple yet significant event gave us an
opportunity to put this truth into practice at
once.

One of us had consecrated herself to God
privately with a vow of chastity. Shortly after,
though, she felt the Lord was calling her to a
total self-giving.

Reflecting on the things she had not yet given
up to the Lord, she thought she should make
a gift of her own will to him through obedience,
renounce her few possessions by living in

poverty, and leave her family and her career by withdrawing altogether from the world. She concluded that God must be calling her to the cloister.

Although she did not feel inclined to embrace that state of life, she uttered her " yes. "

When she confided in her confessor, however, he tried to dissuade her, saying that her apostolate in the world was of greater utility. She obeyed him, and this event made all of us realize that the important thing is not so much the greater or lesser perfection of one vocation or another, but the will of God for us, for each one of us.

We were greatly impressed by the words of St. Francis of Sales: " The soul that loves God is so utterly transformed into His divine will as to deserve to be called the very name, ' God's will.' This is why, through the mouth of the prophet Isaiah, the Lord says that he will call the Christian Church by a new name, which he will deeply impress on the hearts of each one of His faithful, that is, ' My will in him.' The title that will carry the greatest honor for Christians will be: 'God's will in them. ' " [1]

Like many others in the world, we had thought the way of sanctity to be extremely

[1] St. Francis of Sales, *On the Love of God*, Bk. 8, chap. 7.

hard to come by. But now we had before us a way that was wide open to everybody, girls and mothers, priests and workers, children and old people, religious and government officials. This way is called, " the will of God. "

This simple discovery was the source of great joy for us. We felt we now had in our possession a key to sanctity which we could offer to all those we met on our way, and even to the great masses of mankind.

So this became our main task: to strive to incarnate *the will of God for us.* It was in this way that we could translate our ideal into life.

From that moment, two roads seemed to fork out before us. How many years remained to us on earth? Twenty? Thirty? Or just a few days or months? We could either spend this time doing our own will, or that of God. Generally people just follow their own will, and as a result, even when they manage to avoid serious sin, once they have passed away, they're soon forgotten.

Trying, on the other hand, to perform the divine will, offering our souls as a chalice to contain His will, gradually we would no longer live in ourselves, but Christ would live in us.

We might not know where He would lead us, yet it would not be difficult to abandon ourselves in the Lord, in him whom we had now rediscovered as Love itself. The melancholy tone of " resignation " with which we, who call ourselves Christians, say, " Thy will be done," when confronted by difficult situations, now appeared strange and inappropriate. It was not the performance of God's will that called for sad " resignation, "but of our own will, which is so inconclusive and wearying to souls created for what is infinite, for the plan of love that our heavenly Father has prepared for each one of us.

The saints, too, had fulfilled the divine will for them, and this was the secret of their greatness.

In our desire to reach the sanctity that was theirs, we had sometimes, especially at the beginning, imitated their actions rather blindly. Like children who copy the slightest gestures of adults, we had learned from them the various physical and spiritual penances one reads about in books: sleeping on the floor, night vigils, and so forth.

We often used to say that if to become a saint one had to pray, we would pray all day long. If hair shirts were necessary, we'd wear them night and day. If we had to scourge ourselves with chains, we would do even that. What were we to do? What did God want from us?

We came to the conclusion that the saints

were to be imitated above all by doing, as they had always done, the will of God. It was, in fact, the accomplishment of God's will that had made of them God's masterpieces, so that together, they reflected the infinite variety of God, who is Love. Only in this way would even physical and spiritual penances find their true place in our spiritual lives.

God ... to love God by doing his will.

God and his will are one and the same. To persevere in the divine will is to live on in God.

A few simple but helpful illustrations helped clarify these concepts for us.

God is like the sun. A ray from this sun falls on each one of us; that is, the divine will for me, for my companion, for the others. One single sun, sending forth many rays, all of them *sun rays*.

One only God, one will, different for each person, but always his will.

One should keep to one's own ray, and never drift away from it.

And this was to be done in the time given to us: now, later, tomorrow ... carrying out God's will in the present moment, then, in the moment that follows, until we reach the final moment, on which our eternity will depend.

We are not to dwell on the past or dream

about the future. The past should be left to God's mercy, since it is no longer ours; and the future will only be fully lived when it becomes the present.

Only the present is in our hands. So that if God is to reign in our lives, we must concentrate our whole mind, heart and strength on the accomplishment of his will here and now.

Just as a traveler in a train would not think of moving forward through the cars so as to get to his destination sooner, but remains seated and lets the train carry him along, so our souls, to get to God, should fulfill, wholeheartedly, his will in the present moment, since time moves forward on its own.

Nor would it be too hard to understand what God wanted from us. He manifests his will to us through our superiors, through the Scriptures, the demands of our particular state in life, through events around us, personal inspirations, and so on. Moment by moment, helped and enlightened by actual grace, we would build the edifice of our sanctity; or better, while we fulfilled the will of Another—of God himself—he would " build up " himself in us.

At the beginning, however, being somewhat unrehearsed in this life, and obviously unable to ask our spiritual director for advice at every step, we were sometimes in doubt about what the Lord wanted from us.

Whenever we had a choice between two lines of action that were equally good, believing in God's love, and assuring him that we desired his will above all, we would choose one of the two ways, convinced that if it were not what God wanted, he would surely lead us back onto the right path.

Thus, step by step, we learned to listen with increasing attention to that voice within us, which underscored the will of God for us, a will that was manifested in different ways, so that we learned to distinguish this voice from the many other voices of our own will, of the " old man " in us.

We lived this way, certain that with the passing of time, the Lord would, with our lives, weave a marvelous design, like a divine embroidery.

Seen from the world's angle, from a strictly human point of view, its workmanship would appear marred in places by knots, wherever the broken thread ends had to be tied together again. Those would be the occasions when, having departed through human weakness from the ray of the divine will, we would once more return to it, casting ourselves on the mercy of the

Lord. But seen from heaven, as God sees things, where " in everything God works for good with those who love him," the embroidery would be resplendent with the wonderful plan of God's love.

Moreover, our own design would be interlaced with those of others, of all those who had, together with us, done the divine will.

The resulting whole would be the handiwork of God, the only one who knows how to conduct, to order and to harmonize things together in a divine manner.

Later, we were able to see something of all this become a reality.

In the very first months, the Lord impressed on our hearts the main points of the spirituality that was to animate both us and the whole Movement, which was now spreading irresistibly around the initial group.

Then—in the course of these last twenty-five years—the shape of this new movement which God had chosen to raise up in his Church, gradually became clearer to us.

At various moments of our history, those in authority asked for a description of it.

Each time, we tried hard to take from the experience of the Movement the law that appeared to guide it from within. And in spite of many difficulties, the Church encouraged us to continue along the way that we believed to have been indicated by God.

The Church intervened again on a number of occasions, giving us counsel and having us rewrite the Rule several times, until it acquired the form of the 1963 version, which we now possess with gratitude and joy, having received it as God's will from the hands of the Church. The Church's intervention was simply and solely an expression of her love for us: the love of a mother who watches over, respects, and approves the work of her child. And we, in obeying her, feel ourselves to be free children of God.

The will of God! We can say, after all these years, that with God's grace we have believed in love, and that God has not let us down.

Today our Movement, now officially recognized and approved, advances—alongside the thousands of other movements that exist in the Church—in its journey through the years and, let us hope, through the centuries, along the track of the divine will.

IV

A New Law for a New City

WHEN A PERSON EMIGRATES to a distant land, especially if it is less developed than his own, he carries with him his own customs and practices. No doubt he adapts himself, whenever necessary, to the new environment, but often he continues to use his mother tongue, to dress in ways long familiar to him, and to construct buildings like those of his own land.

When the Word of God became man, he certainly adapted himself to the manner of life of this world. He was first a child, then an exemplary son, a grown man, and a worker. But he also brought with him the manner of life of his own homeland in heaven, for he desired that men and things should be constituted in a new order, according to the law of heaven, the law of love.

These were our thoughts while still under the terror and affliction of the war.

And perhaps this is why, when we lovingly opened the Gospels or other books of the New Testament, during the long hours of waiting in the shelter, the verses that particularly stood out were those that more explicitly speak about love. " Only one thing is needful." " Love your neighbor as yourself." " Love your enemies." " Love one another." " Above all things have a constant mutual charity."

These words seemed to possess a revolutionary force, a hitherto unsuspected vitality. They were the only words capable of radically changing the lives of men, even of us, Christians of today.

But while realizing that the basic principle of the Gospel is charity, and that this is the bond of perfection, we did not immediately see how it was that we should live it, nor with whom and to what degree we were to practice it.

At the beginning, due mainly to the distressing circumstances of the war, we directed our love toward the poor, convinced that in those lean and at times repulsive faces, we could discern the face of the Lord.

It was a real school of training. We had not, in the past, been accustomed to loving others supernaturally. At most, we had cultivated relationships of respect or friendship with our relatives or friends which, however admirable, did not distinguish us in any way from people who do not share our faith.

But now, under the impulse of grace, trusting in God and in his Providence—which cares for the birds of the air and the flowers of the field— we got down to looking after the poor of the city. We invited them to our houses, to our tables. It was a great honor for us to be able to offer them the first place at table, the finest cutlery, the best food. When we could not receive them in our homes, we arranged to meet them at street corners and handed them whatever we had managed to put together for their needs. We called on them in their dismal shacks and helped them out with medical provisions.

The poor were truly the object of our love. We loved Jesus through them and, indeed, in them. Moreover, all those who had been attracted by our common ideal, also shared in caring for them. As the community grew around the initial nucleus, there increased the possibilities of helping the poor and relieving their suffering. It was a wonderful spectacle which seemed more the work of angels than of men. Hundreds of packages of food, clothing and medicine were distributed in such abundance that, especially during those final years of the war, it certainly looked like a special intervention of divine Providence.

Every now and then small but significant events occurred which, because of their supernatural savor, strengthened our souls and served as a confirmation that the Lord was with us.

With faith we would pray before the Blessed Sacrament: " Lord, give me a pair of shoes, size 10 . . . for you," meaning " for you in that poor man who needs them."

" Lord, give me a man's jacket . . . for you."

And it wasn't rare that upon leaving the church, a friend would come up and offer us what we had asked for.

Such things as these occur to any follower of Christ who is familiar with the truth of the words: " Ask, and it will be given you." But, nevertheless, they never ceased to fill us with wonder; while, at the same time, we were spurred on by those other, extraordinary experiences in the lives of our great brothers who had preceded us and who also knew—at a time when they were not yet saints—the difficulties encountered in the ascent to God, in the process of thawing our hardened human personalities in the fire of divine love.

We knew that when St. Catherine of Siena, in her love for the poor, gave to one her mantle

50

and to another her cross, Jesus had appeared to her on the following nights to thank her for the gifts she had made him in the person of the poor man.

St. Francis is said to have given away his cloak to the poor on some thirty different occasions.

Surely, then, it was no great sacrifice for us to remove our gloves in winter and to offer them to somebody who was forced to beg for hours out in the cold, in the snow, simply to keep body and soul together.

The exercise of charity, moreover, awoke in us a desire for a greater social justice among men.

We possessed certain things. The poor did not.

The rich have. The destitute have not.

Why not spontaneously deprive ourselves of whatever was not strictly necessary for our basic needs—we who could surely always find something or other that we could give away—to help those who were dying for lack of food, or freezing from the cold, so as to raise their standard of living with the thousand little acts of assistance that charity prompts us to perform?

We tried to do this.

The Movement at this time already counted several hundred people, and since about thirty of these were actually suffering from hunger, the others undertook to make as generous a monthly contribution as possible on their behalf, while at the same time attempts were made to procure regular jobs for them. It could really be said, as was once said of the first Christians: " There was not a needy person among them."

This activity was vigorously kept up for several months.

Yet, in spite of the great generosity of people individually, we were aware that something more than this would be needed to relieve the wants of the poor part of society. We began to see that this, perhaps, was not the immediate goal for which the Lord had moved us to perform concrete works of charity.

But it was only later that we began to understand what the Lord's specific purpose was in leading us in this direction: it is in charity, through the practice of charity, that one can better comprehend the things of heaven, and that God can more easily enlighten our souls.

It was probably this exercise in love that enabled us to see that our hearts must be opened not only toward the poor, but toward all people without any distinction whatever.

No doubt there were people who needed to be fed, to be given drink, to be clothed, but there were also those who had to be instructed, counseled, comforted, or who were in need of prayers.

Opportunities to practice the corporal and spiritual works of mercy then fanned out in every direction before us. These, above all, would form the substance of the very definite questions that the judge of our lives would ask in deciding our eternal destiny. And the thought that Jesus, in his infinite love, had revealed this fact when he came on earth in order to facilitate our entry into heaven, filled us with a sense of adoration.

We all of us wanted to respond with our love to his great love for us by putting this will of his into effect.

God was not asking us to love only the poor, but each and every neighbor, whoever he might be, as we love ourselves.

So if we came across someone who was weeping, we tried to weep with him, that his cross might be lightened. If somebody was happy, we tried to be happy with him, and the joy was all the greater. " Rejoice with those who rejoice, weep with those who weep. "

This was what being Christians meant. This, we realized, was the true life. It was in the constant living of this charity toward every person we met—rich or poor, educated or not, man or woman, adult or child, white or colored—that we appreciated more deeply than ever the truth of the words of Scripture: " We have passed out of death into life, because we love the brethren."

Since at that time we met with obvious difficulties—living in close contact while being full of imperfections—we decided to look at one another, not in a merely human way, noticing the speck in the other's eye and disregarding the beam in one's own, but forgiving and forgetting all things. We considered this effort to forgive one another, as God in his mercy did with us, such a vital duty, that we promised, with a kind of pact of mercy, to try to see the others upon getting up each morning, as *new*, that is, without any of the defects we had previously observed in them.

What impressed us especially was the beauty and novelty of Jesus' command to love our enemies, be they close or distant.

It meant turning the other cheek and walking for two miles, as the Gospel says: " If anyone strikes you on the right cheek, turn to him the other also . . . and if anyone forces you to go for one mile, go with him two miles. "

This we were ready to do, should we have come across any hostile person along our way.

And finally . . . the pearl of the Good Tidings, the commandment of mutual love.

" A new commandment I give to you, that you love one another; even as I have loved you, that you also love one another."

As Jesus had loved us? What was the measure of his love for us? His death on the cross. We should be ready, then, to die for one another, since " greater love has no man than this, that a man lay down his life for his friends."

And if giving our own life was the measure, then surely we should be prepared to satisfy any lesser demand on our love by a neighbor, be it small or large.

We should be ready to give away our material possessions . . . .

One day we took our few, modest belongings from the wardrobe and piled them up in the middle of the room. Then we gave each one the few things she needed, and what was left over we distributed to the poor.

Our earnings, too, we should be ready to share together, as well as all the trifles or valuables we had, or would one day come to possess . . . .

We should also be prepared to share our spiritual possessions . . . .

Our very desire for personal sanctity had

taken second place in favor of the single-minded choice of God, a choice that excluded every other objective, yet did include, obviously, the sanctity that God had in mind for each one of us.

We accordingly communicated to one another the positive experiences which this new life brought with it: fruits of charity, which always produces new light in the soul. We did this out of love, for we desired that this should be our only debt to one another: " Owe no one anything, except to love one another."

Even Jesus, after all, when he came on earth, had said: " All that I have heard from my Father I have made known to you " (John 15, 15).

This communication of spiritual things for one another's mutual benefit, as prudence and circumstances allowed, became a feature especially of the life of those who were called to live in community, being a practical expression of the words of Scripture: " Our conversation is in heaven." Previously there were days when we languished in boredom and tended to live in a purely natural manner. Now, however, our time was filled with talk of the things of God, thus satisfying a deep longing we had felt in our hearts to find a way of spending our whole lives in and for God, without losing a single moment. Gradually, and by means, too, of our reciprocal help, the Lord—" where charity and love are, there is God "—began to distinguish more and more clearly the thoughts, desires and fruits of the " old man " in us from those of " the new man."

Then there echoed in our souls with an altogether new ring the words, " You were taught . . . to put on the new man, which has been created according to God in justice and holiness of truth."

God is love, but he is also light. And Jesus is the light that has come into the world (John 1, 9-10).

The more we love, the more we *see*.

While 1943 was the year when the Movement began, 1949 marked an especially significant step forward.

Circumstances that were quite normal, though nonetheless providential, made it possible for those who formed the initial nucleus of the Movement to retire from their everyday surroundings and go up to the Dolomite mountains for a period of rest.

We were withdrawing from contact with people, but we could in no way abandon the way of life which now constituted the very reason for our existence.

The poverty of a small, rustic mountain house provided us with shelter.

We were alone, just the few of us together, with our great Ideal lived out moment by moment; with Jesus in the Eucharist, the bond of unity, to whom we had daily recourse; alone in our rest, our prayer and meditation.

And there, a time of special graces began.

We had the impression that the Lord opened the eyes of our soul to the kingdom of God in our midst: the Trinity indwelling in a small cell of the Mystical Body. "Father, that they may be one even as we are one." And it seemed to us that the work of God that was then starting would be none other than a mystical presence of Mary within the Church.

Understandably, we would not have come down from that mountain, the little Tabor of our souls, if the will of God had not demanded differently. It was only through our love for Jesus crucified and forsaken, living in a humanity plunged in darkness, that we found the courage to descend.

In 1950 and 1951, we went back to the same place in the mountains and there, immersed once more in " the things of heaven," we hardly noticed that the number of people who gathered in the valley was steadily increasing from year to year. There were no longer just young women, but mothers, fathers, young men and children.

In the following years we had to rent buildings in four small neighboring towns in order to accommodate all the people who came.

In 1951 this yearly gathering began to be referred to as a " city."

Charity was the basic law of this living community; it was also the only requirement for admission.

One could not go there as a passive observer, but had to take an active part along with the others in " building " this mystical city so filled with joy. Here all competed in the service of one another and were willing to endure even considerable hardship and discomfort in order to take part.

In '52, '53 and '54, a new feature was the presence, in large numbers, of secular priests and of religious belonging to a great variety of orders, the different spiritualities harmonizing together, with each one shining out all the more splendidly in this common brotherhood.

At the end of every summer, after this time spent together in mutual and constant charity, and in the service of all men, the Lord would make clearer to those responsible, certain new aspects of the Movement, which then served to shape the program for that coming year.

In 1955 the " city " was first named " Mariapolis " (" City of Mary ").

In 1956 the presence of representatives from five continents made us feel more acutely the need for all of us to remain in contact, even after our departure, whatever our destination might be, so as to help each other persevere in this spirit.

With this end in view, the periodical *Città Nuova* (" New City ") was founded, as an expression of mutual charity. It was this same motive that led, shortly after, to its publication in all the principal languages.

In 1957 the Mariapolis was visited not only by some persons widely known for their activities in the Church, but also by many bishops, who felt themselves in a climate of the living Church.

In 1958 an international exhibition, at which all the latest scientific and technological inventions were displayed, gave us the idea of making our Mariapolis that year a little " Expo' of God, " where the values of the spirit might be spotlighted.

And finally 1959. By then the Mariapolis was like a flower in full bloom. It was a small model of that city of Mary which the Movement would henceforth contribute to building in many parts of the world.

There were people from twenty-seven countries, representing nine different languages. In oneness of spirit they consecrated their respective home-lands to God, thus expressing their desire to form, together, *the people of God.*

In later years we were to see people highly impressed, and sometimes even converted, by an account of this 1959 Mariapolis, or by a simple documentary on it.

We have often asked ourselves the reason for this widespread, attraction. Why did the Mariapolis draw and fascinate people in this way? Its influence has crossed the mountains and seas. Without exaggeration one may say that it has reached the four corners of the earth. The reason we thought must be this: just as with Mary it is not so much her own self that shines forth, but the presence of God in her heart, so too, the " good fragrance " of Christ that these meetings help to spread far and wide, is to be attributed not so much to the coming together of people of many races and nations, of different ages and social condi-tions, but to God himself, present in the midst of the Christian community whenever constant and mutual charity is practiced by all.

As a result of these meetings innumerable people have come to believe and the hearts of many have begun to beat with renewed vigor. Heaven alone knows how many souls have, through God's mercy, experienced a spiritual rebirth simply because a certain number of people came together from all parts of the world, as brothers and sisters, and bore witness to God, offering their hearts to him so that the kingdom of God might be brightly visible among them.

At the end of the summer, after all had left, the echo came from the cities and the most out-of-the-way towns, from people who let it be known that they had experienced the presence of their Lord, that they had found God and that life was something totally different now.

Many wept upon leaving. It was as if, once back in the world, they felt themselves to be orphans again, but with a childlike faith and hope that heaven would somehow let them see that dream again and, with omnipotent hand, would make it spread all over the globe.

If it is true to say that these gatherings were attended by people who came from every walk of life, married and single, men and women of every kind, lay people and priests, rich and poor ... it is also true that when they departed, they left along every road, for the Mariapolis aroused vocations of all sorts, even the most arduous, in the hearts of many who went there.

It was like a city set high on a mountain, which many were able to see.

People saw for themselves and exclaimed: " This is what the whole world should be like."

Of this splendid flower of the Church— generated from, within, and because of Jesus' new commandment—we felt that we could say, as St. Augustine once said:

> What Babel dispersed
> The Church gathers in.
> One language became many;
> Do not wonder,
> This was the work of pride.
> Many languages became one;
> Do not marvel,
> This was the fruit of love.

Now, at a distance of some ten years from the last Mariapolis held in the Dolomites, we can observe that each year, these short-term cities have been growing up in increasing numbers, in such widely separated countries as Chile and Korea, Australia and Paraguay, the United States and the Philippines. The more than thirty

Mariapolis gatherings that are presently held each year make it possible for people around the globe to live a few days in an atmosphere replete with the beauty of God. In Italy, moreover, a permanent city is rising up from this " template," a lasting monument to Jesus' new commandment. And this offspring of the Movement, too, as we can already gather, will not be the only one of its kind.

V

The Key to Union

JUST AS ALL OF CHRISTIANITY is a mystery of love and suffering, so too the truly vital elements in our movement are love and suffering.

And just as in Christianity love generally overcomes suffering and life is victor over death, so it is, also, in the Movement.

When we started out on this new life we sometimes wondered what the most beautiful thing in the world might be: whether the stars, or flowers, or children, or men of genius, or sunsets .... And we arrived at the conclusion that the most beautiful thing is love, the maternal, fraternal and conjugal forms of love that God has placed in the human heart.

Jesus himself raised fraternal love to a supernatural level, making of all Christians a single brotherhood. The love of a mother seemed to us even more beautiful, since, purified by sorrow, it is more lasting and more sacred to the human heart. Yet conjugal love appeared to excel over almost every other kind of love, for it makes it possible for two creatures to abandon all other natural bonds of affection in order to found a new family.

Love is certainly a wonderful thing. " But—we wondered—what must God be like who created it? And shall we, who have left all things for his sake, be able to experience, in this life, something of the love that is God? " We often read the writings of the saints, whom we got to know one by one. They were the real experts in the love of God. They were authentic Christians who, precisely because they were such, had experienced this love while still on earth.

St. Clare of Assisi, after praying at great length before the crucifix in the church of St. Damian's, on rejoining her companions would speak to them of the things of heaven, her face all radiant with a light that she had derived from the contemplation of the divine, suffering figure on the cross.

St. Bonaventure, in his *Stimulus of Divine Love,* teaches that to reach the heart of Christ, the furnace of God's love, we must first pass through his wounds.

The soul of St. Catherine of Siena seemed wholly concentrated on two concepts: fire and blood. She felt herself to be almost identified with the very Fire of Christ's love. She once said to her companions: " I am the fire, you are the sparks," and she used other highly expressive terms that pointed out to us the necessity of passing through suffering in order to " burn " with this love. In one of her letters she writes: " Clothe yourselves in the Blood, bathe in the Blood, immerse yourselves in the Blood, drown yourselves in the Blood, inebriate yourselves in the Blood."

Every saint is different from all the others, possessing a strongly marked personality of his own. But each one has ultimately found this Love by walking along the solemn way of the Passion of Christ.

One day we heard a priest, speaking on the suffering of Christ, say that perhaps the moment when Jesus suffered most was on Calvary when he cried out: " My God, my God, why have you forsaken me? "

Commenting on these words when we got home we decided, in our desire to live well the one life we had, to choose *Jesus forsaken*—as we called him in his suffering—as our Model.

And from that moment on, he, his face, his mysterious cry, seemed to color every moment of suffering in our lives.

We too, like everybody else, at times experienced spiritual states of affliction that might be described as darkness, aridity, a sense of failure, loneliness, the heaviness of our own human nature, of our sins.

But was not Jesus, at the ninth hour, immersed in a blackness so thick that it infinitely surpassed any feelings of darkness that we might ever have?

And was not this aridity so great that his divine soul seemed temporarily deprived of the loving presence of the Father?

He, the victorious one, never appeared such a great failure as at that moment. But it was then that he, the Son of God, indivisibly one with him, reunited all the children to their Father by paying the price of this most terrible desolation. He, the completely innocent one, took upon his shoulders the weight of all our sins, drawing down upon himself and absorbing, like a divine lightning conductor, the full force of God's justice.

While at first we had sluggishly dragged ourselves through moments of suffering, waiting for something unexpected to turn up that would help to make the difficulty pass, now, in similar circumstances, seeing our little sorrows in the shadow of his, we stood firm, withdrawing into the depths of our souls so as to offer this suffering to Jesus, happy to add our little droplet to the sea of his pain. An then we would continue to live moment by moment, wholeheartedly performing his will, as for example, by loving the neighbor that circumstances brought our way.

Doing this, our spiritual darkness, the sense of failure, aridity, all these disappeared, and we began to understand how dynamically divine is the Christian life, which knows nothing of emptiness, or the cross, or suffering, except as things that pass, and which enables us to experience the fullness of life, meaning resurrection and light and hope, even in the midst of tribulations.

Later we were to learn that there are certain forms of aridity that affect one profoundly and produce real nights of the soul, true foretastes of purgatory that may last for months or even years.

At such times, for instance, the person can no longer see, so to speak, its Spouse before it. By a special privilege of his love, Christ wishes to purify and prepare the soul to serve him in his work by identifying it with his own suffering, not even leaving it, as someone has well said, the strength to offer, but only to suffer.

All this, however, did not apply to us, since we were then just beginners in this life.

For all of us, then, Jesus forsaken was the key that invariably opened the way to union with God.

He was also the means whereby we remedied any small imperfections in the unity that had been established among us through " a constant mutual charity."

" Where charity and love are, there is God." Where love and charity are wanting, therefore, God is not present. And there were times when his consoling presence, which gave meaning to the new life we had set out upon, casting a new light on even the smallest acts performed out of love for him, clarifying for us the things that happened in the present and making us see the future as bright and beckoning . . . there were times when all this vanished. This fullness of joy that results when unity is achieved among men was lost as a consequence of the pride or egoism of one or another, of an attachment to one's own ideas or belongings, or because of a failure in charity.

Our souls would then experience confusion. They reeled about in the dark, and any progress made up till then seemed unavailing. It was as if the sun of our luminous unity had set.

Then, only the memory of Jesus in his profound abandonment, of the darkness in which his soul had been engulfed, gave us hope that all was not lost. On the contrary, our present state, being one of suffering, could actually be pleasing to God if offered to him out of love. And we strove to do this, courageously bringing about unity again by asking pardon and taking the initiative, even when it was the other who had something against us. The Gospel warned us that not even our offering at the altar was pleasing to God in a climate void of reciprocal charity.

So the sun would shine once more in our little community, the presence of Jesus among those who are united in his name.

Through love for Jesus forsaken, light and peace reigned not only in our souls, but also in the souls of all those who, being lonely, disorientated, orphaned, disillusioned, failures in life, downcast, desperate, helpless or caught up in a meaningless existence, reminded us, in one way or another, of him whom we had chosen. Such persons were sought out by the members of the Movement, who tried to share with them the troubles that filled their hearts. And then, at the right moment, they would speak to them of Jesus, of his infinite love, of his favor for

71

the categories of people mentioned in the beatitudes, of the privilege that was theirs in being able to help him carry his cross, for their own good and that of humanity. They also explained how one must offer Him personal sorrows, always recognizing in them, the countenance of Christ.

Had not Theresa of Lisieux, when she first discovered the sickness from which she eventually died, exclaimed: " Here is the Spouse "?

In this way we gradually learned, we and all our friends, that suffering is always sacred. We were not merely to put up with it, but to actually embrace it.

So our solitude was filled with God, and with the presence of the many others who by then belonged to the Movement. In Christ forsaken, souls found an orientation for their lives. In contact with people who were all trying to do God's will, orphans, for example, found not only brothers and sisters, but fathers and mothers. The disillusioned and the weary, those who have been defeated by life, found an answer to their problems. The *why* of each one found an answer in his great *why*.

With the Incarnation, Jesus was right down at our own level; but on the cross he was crushed, and in his abandonment he seemed to be altogether annihilated. Acting as a divine, inclined plane, he made it possible for *any* man on earth, *whatever* his moral and spiritual state, to ascend to God's divine Majesty, on condition that he turn to Christ and following the example of Christ, transform the whole of his oppressive burden of sorrow into the pure gold of love.

Thus, in the course of time, many people, by means of our Movement too, have understood or experienced the truth of the words of Jesus: " Those who are well have no need of a physician, but those who are sick."

And every morning we, so as to be true Christians, repeated to ourselves on rising: " Because you are forsaken ... " as if to say: " You, Lord, crucified, are the reason for my life, under whatever form you appear. I will not shirk this encounter with you. No, I will consider it the most precious moment of the day."

Around us were also atheists, those far from God, desecrated tabernacles, yet members of the Mystical Body, or at any rate orientated towards it.

In these brothers, also, we recognized his image.

It was this love for Jesus forsaken in them, and the testimony of unity among ourselves, that worked, with the grace of God, the most varied conversions.

There are works in the Church that do not bear visible fruit, because the supernatural good they do is mysteriously destined to reach that part of the Mystical Body which God knows to be most in need. Other organizations are dedicated to the performance of works of mercy, raising up schools, orphanages, hospitals, etc.

The function of the Movement consists, through God's grace, in bringing about the conversion of individuals, a full change of heart and mind, and in helping to lead back to God the whole of the society in which it is immersed.

The love of Jesus forsaken was also our means for the diffusion of this ideal in the world.

There is no case in which the seed of grain, cast into the earth, does not need to die and decay in order to bear much fruit. This fact was borne out every time the Movement made some advance, no matter where.

The trials were of various kinds, little or great " agonies " to which it was never easy to get accustomed.

But did not Jesus crucified, burdened under the weight of our sins, show himself to be the divine seed of grain that withers and dies to give us the life of the sons of God?

It was in his name, for love of him, that we accepted these trials, thus contributing to the conversion of the world to God.

Whenever this young tree, then, had taken root, here and there in new regions and nations, other trials would come along that reminded us of the " prunings " spoken of in the Gospel. These sometimes led to changes in one part or another of the Focolare Movement, which were often accompanied by much suffering. But if this suffering was accepted out of love, it always procured a greater good.

And for that matter, was not Jesus, in his abandonment, " pruned " by heaven itself, so as to give to men, separated from God, the possibility of regrafting themselves in him?

Furthermore, looking beyond the confines of the Movement, which was then burgeoning, we sought to see and to love him also in the great sufferings of the Church.

We saw him particularly in those sections of the Mystical Body that are impoverished by secularism, or by materialism and atheism, and are often ill-treated and martyred, undergoing subtle and atrocious forms of persecution. This part of the Church, which seemed to resound with Jesus' cry, " My God, my God, why have you forsaken me, " captured our interest. It awak-

ened in us a vocation: to bring God where he
is in want.

Divisions within the faith appeared to us as
a gaping wound in the Mystical Body. It is well
known that among Christians not of the Roman
Catholic confession, there has existed for some
time a widespread ecumenical movement that
aspires to unity. It seemed that the Lord wished
to make use of the Movement, too, on a vast
scale, to help break down age-long prejudices,
and to stimulate mutual knowledge and esteem
as a necessary first step toward future unity.

There are also portions of the Mystical Body
wasting away for lack of spiritual nourishment.
In a place like Latin America, there are very
few to care for the spiritual needs of a population
that is overwhelmingly Christian. These people
are our brothers, who have inherited the same
faith, yet they find themselves in circumstances
that make it almost impossible for them to
maintain this faith. They, too, reminded us of
Jesus forsaken.

Throughout the world, from missionary lands
to the still pagan areas where Christ is unknown,
mankind seemed to be waiting for one thing: the
Gospel, which alone enables men to find their
true selves, because it reveals to them the

Creator, in whom all things have meaning and value.

All these peoples, whether pagan or not, seemed to send out a cry of abandonment to which we had to respond, if we were to react in these circumstances as Christ himself would, he who must live in us today, in the twentieth century, with all its special needs and problems.

Putting its trust in God, the Movement wished to help meet these urgent needs of humanity, and there was no better way of doing this than to try to relive, step by step, the words that Jesus uttered when, for the sake of humanity, he was among men; to believe and to practice, with utter conviction, the things he taught, and to make our own the prayer which is both his program and his final testament: " Father, that they may all be one."

For this reason the Movement has always tried to keep in contact with all those in the world who know and live this spirit.

With the help of God's grace we would like to have for each person the same love that Jesus had for his disciples (" And having loved his own . . . he loved them to the end.") so that all of us together may form, in Christ who has called us, an ever denser network throughout the world. In this way each one may be helped to persevere and, trustingly, courageously, to overcome his trials with the aid of all the others, while at the same time giving a witness to the Gospel and the Church before as many people as possible, since Jesus prayed for all men, with none excluded.

This is our ideal: Jesus crucified and forsaken, in us and outside of us, in the whole world that is waiting to be consoled and comforted.

From our limited experience we have learned that there is no true Christian life except in those who have fully embraced the cross, for ours is one of the innumerable possible actualizations of the words of Jesus: " If any man would come after me, let him deny himself and take up his cross and follow me."

But by way of comfort to those who embark for the first time upon this divine adventure, we can say that, in a small way, we too, like our giant brothers the saints, have experienced the truth that in casting oneself into the arms of the cross, one finds not only suffering, but love, the love that is the life of God himself within us.

VI

Words of Life

FROM THE VERY BEGINNING of the Movement
one of its characteristic features has been
the practice of the *word of life*.

One of the first group, in her previous experience, had sincerely and ardently searched for
the truth, thinking it necessary to delve deeply
into the philosophies, essentially positivist in
tendency, that were then being taught in schools.
This she had done while continuing, in all good
faith, to live as a devout and practicing Christian.

But now, as the war raged, we made a new
" discovery, " simple yet far-reaching in its impli-
cations: Jesus himself is the Truth. If we wished
to attain to the truth, then, we should follow
him, the Word incarnate.

And it was in the Gospel, verse by verse,
word by word, that we would find his teaching.

We used to gather in a little circle in the
damp, rocky shelters and, by the light of a

candle, lovingly read the divine book. The words
we found there shone out before the eyes of our
souls with a rare brilliance. Never before had
the Gospel been so singular and engrossing to
us; never as then, had it seemed so new.

Written with a divine realism and perfection,
it offered to us *words of life,* words that could
be translated into life. By comparison with them,
the words of even the most outstanding devo-
tional writings seemed watered down; while
those that filled our books of high learning, of
philosophy, seemed to fade away into the shadows.
The word of God had a wide, a universal, range
of application.

We, our friends, and people of all kinds, dark-
or light-skinned, those who lived three centuries
ago and those of a century hence, mothers and
members of parliament, landworkers and prison-
ers, grandfathers and grandsons, every man
born into this world could live the word of
God, every word of God.

" Unless your righteousness exceeds that of the
scribes and pharisees, you will never enter the
kingdom of heaven." Forgive " seventy times
seven." " Give to every man who asks .... "

Jesus is truly a light " that enlightens every
man who comes into the world."

God's becoming man was no ordinary event,

nor was it given to us to listen to words of eternal life at any time we choose.

It was expedient and logical to listen, during this brief span of life at our disposal, to the divine words that Jesus had spoken precisely for us, for men, and to put them into practice.

The conviction God had given us in this regard was deeply rooted, and we felt an urgent need to act upon it. We desired to live in such a way that if, hypothetically speaking, all the copies of the Gospels in the world were destroyed, people observing our conduct would, in some manner, be able to reconstruct them: " Blessed are those who mourn . . . . " Blessed are the merciful . . . . " " Judge not . . . . " Love your enemies . . . . "

Every week we concentrated on living a particular phrase of the Gospel.

We carried it in our hearts like a treasure and applied it whenever possible.

Furthermore, living in mutual and constant charity, and wishing to share even our spiritual riches in order to contribute to the sanctity of the other as much as our own, we told each other of the various ways we had tried to live this phrase, of the consequences that followed, and of our wonderment and joy at seeing our lives changed as a result. We gradually came

to realize how worldly and un-Christian our
previous way of life had been. We were Catholics, yet our mentality was very different from
that of Christ.

" As you did it to one of these the least of
my brethren, you did it to me." Jesus wished to
be loved in others, even in the least of men.

The numerous, yet basically similar consider-
ations we had previously indulged in with regard
to our neighbor, as being pleasant or unpleasant,
handsome or ugly, dull or amusing, old or young,
were swept away by a single concept: it is Jesus
we must love in each one. We were to keep his
image clearly before us; we were to treat our
brother as we would have wanted Jesus to be
treated.

Our faith in the teaching authority of the
Church—strengthened now by the phrase of Holy
Scripture, " He who hears you hears me "—and
our awareness that it is easy to err, even with
the best intentions, especially in the area of the
Scriptures, led us to submit a short written com-
mentary on the weekly " word of life " to our
archbishop for his approval, so that he would
correct it and confirm it.

Ours, in a way, was an " interpretation " of
the Gospel, but it was such in the sense that
an actor, for example, interprets a script prepared

by another person, and under the direction of a third.

Our job was to *live* the Gospel, of Luke, Matthew, etc., to live it *today,* under the guidance of the Church, so as gradually to become other Christs, in our age, in whatever place God had put us.

This we were to do not only by virtue of the supernatural grace possessed by all who are not in a state of mortal sin, but through a progressive re-modeling of our lives according to the Gospel.

A man might remain illiterate up to the age of ninety for lack of a simple knowledge of the alphabet and of a few rules of grammar. A Christian could not be another Jesus, and express his spirit, unless he listened to the words of God and put them into effect. It was vital that we learned to live them, one by one.

In the years that followed, living this way, we came across an infinite number of treasures in the Gospel.

By practicing prudence, simplicity, purity, poverty mercy, etc., we arrived at a more profound and exact conception of charity. While on the other hand, all these virtues tended to become more meaningful and to acquire their proper value as expressions of the love of God and neighbor.

This experience was such a vivid one, that after being nourished for a long period on the word of God, it seemed to us that every word uttered by Christ was nothing other than *love*. It was as if each phrase had exactly the same value as every other, and as if each were the equivalent of Christ's last will, his new commandment of mutual charity. Just as the whole of Jesus was present, not only in the entire Sacred Host, but also in every small particle of it, so also he was present, not only in the whole Gospel, but in each one of the phrases he uttered.

This experience also helped us understand the Church in a new way.

Jesus was the Word of God incarnate.

The Church appeared to us as the Gospel incarnate, and therefore, Spouse of Christ.

Innumerable religious orders had sprung forth through the centuries. Each order, or religious family, could be seen as the " incarnation " of an aspect of the life of Jesus, of an attitude or an event in his life, a particular sorrow, or a single expression that he used.

Solely by their mode of life the Franciscans continued to preach to the world: " Blessed are the poor in spirit, for theirs is the kingdom of heaven."

The Dominicans contemplated the Logos, the Word of God, and simultaneously explained and spread the truth.

The Jesuits emphasized obedience.

St. Theresa of Lisieux and the followers of her " little way " seemed to personify and to hold up permanently before the eyes of men the words: " Unless you turn and become like children, you will never enter the kingdom of heaven."

The Sisters of Bethlehem, of Bethany, of Nazareth were concrete expressions of a period in the life of Jesus; the Stigmatines were a living reminder of his wounds; St. Catherine of Siena, of the blood of Christ; St. Margaret Mary Alacoque, of the Sacred Heart.

Monks combined contemplation with activity.

The Carmelites adored God on Tabor, ever ready to descend in order to preach and face, if need be, their passion and death.

Missionaries lived the precept: " Go into all the world and preach the Gospel to the whole creation."

There were orders, congregations and institutes of charity that followed the example of the good Samaritan.

Just as, in the white snow, water crystalizes into lots of little stars, so also love, which in Jesus assumed its highest expression, the highest kind of beauty, took on diverse forms within the Church in the various orders and religious families.

All the virtues had flowered, and continued to flower, in the splendid garden of the Church.

Each founder of a religious order seemed to us like the personification of a particular virtue. Each, transfigured by much love and suffering, had finally entered into heaven as a living " word of God."

They had fulfilled God's plan for them. So of them, too, it could be said: " Though heaven and earth should pass away, my words will stand." The saints were, and remain to this day, words of God spoken to the world. Made one with his words, they too shall stand.

The whole Church could thus be seen as a majestic Christ manifested down through the centuries and visible across the face of the earth, for the spiritual children of all these saints, by virtue of the Christian blood that runs in their veins, have multiplied and spread wherever in the world the Church of God is present.

From the start of the Movement, men and women religious of almost every existing order have expressed a willingness to adhere to it's spirit, considering it beneficial also for them.

In the emphasis put by the Movement on evangelical charity, the cross, the spirit of unity, Holy Scripture, the blessed Virgin, the Church, the Mystical Body, they saw a revival of the very concepts which, in one way or another, had inspired their own founders.

The encounter with the Movement and the practice of its spirituality not only increased their zeal for God's glory, but led them to a deeper appreciation of their own Rules, and to a greater love and a clearer understanding of their founders.

This deeper comprehension of their common father, the founder, was naturally followed by a strengthening of the bond that united them together. The spirit of the Movement, properly interpreted and practiced, led to a more loving and genuine spirit of obedience toward superiors, so much so that the fruits of this were quickly manifest.

Certain orders, for instance, through a more careful observance of their own internal rules, underwent a real process of renovation. Sometimes there was a revival of their primitive observance; there were increases in vocations; new developments in the mission fields; those who lived this spirit were often entrusted with difficult and responsible assignments; a new wave of life entered many seminaries.

The 1959 Mariapolis was attended by members of sixty religious orders, to mention only those for men. All of them were united by a single purpose, to live consciously as members of the Mystical Body.

Mary, who certainly was spiritually present in her own city, seemed to cover with her mantle all these different religious habits, which often served to give even an outward expression to the particular ideal pursued by each order.

It seemed that Mary, the mother of all men, wished, by means of this Movement, to serve her son Jesus in many different dwellings of the Church, by leading the members of many different religious communities to feel that they belonged, yes, to their own orders, but above all to the one Church.

All this came about quite spontaneously within the Movement, and a result was the formation of a special center to serve all those living a life of consecration to God.

When Jesus said: " Where two or three are gathered in my name, there am I in the midst of them," he certainly did not mean to exclude a Franciscan with a Benedictine, or a Carmelite with a Passionist, or a Jesuit with a Dominican.

And if Jesus is in their midst, this encounter with him will make the Franciscan a better Franciscan, the Dominican a better Dominican, and so forth.

In this way, the Focolare Movement, too, could help make the Church shine forth, in its marvellous variety and profound unity, as a more beautiful and worthy Spouse of Christ.

VII

Jesus in Our Midst

THE WAY THAT THE LORD INDICATED to us from the very beginning was *the way of charity,* evangelical charity, the charity of which St. Paul speaks when he says that it believes all, hopes all, bears all, never thinks evil, is patient . . . .

We began to understand, in fact, that even our own personal sanctification would be achieved by loving others as ourselves. It was this that would ensure our progress through the various stages of the spiritual life. We were being called to share not only our material possessions, but also spiritual things, such as, our own experiences, humbly offering our brethren the essence and the product of the new man in us.

By the fact that several of us, at almost the same time, felt we were being called to embrace the same manner of life, it was toward one another that we practiced it, so that in a short span of time we grasped and put into effect the new commandment of Jesus: " Love one another as I have loved you."

It became increasingly evident that God was urging us to search for his kingdom not only within ourselves, but also in our midst. We would make the kingdom grow within us by trying to establish it among ourselves. The journey toward God was not to be made alone, but together. We were not to seek to become saints on our own, but in company with others, with many others.

And since often in the past we, who were Christians, had possessed an idea of sanctity that made it out to be something wonderful and great, but could contain a certain amount of spiritual egoism, we were grateful to God that he had opened up a way that was new to us, a *way of charity*—and charity is, in fact, *the bond of perfection.*

Today, this way indicated to us by the Lord, might be described as a " collective " way, one to be followed together.

Just as two poles of opposite electrical charge produce light only when they are put into contact, similarly, the uniting of our individual souls by mutual charity produced a new experience. This we felt must be the meaning contained in the words of the Gospel, " Where two or three are gathered in my name, there am I in the midst of them."

Jesus, our brother par excellence, was spiritually present in our midst.

Only he gave meaning to our newly found brotherly relationships. It would surely not have been worthwhile leaving our own fathers, mothers, brothers, sisters, our natural families, pleasing as they are to God, unless it were to belong to a supernatural family with Jesus in our midst.

It was his presence among us that helped us understand the significance of the words in his priestly prayer: " That they may all be one."

It seems to us, in fact, that only with " Jesus in our midst " can the unity invoked by Christ before his death be fully realized.

Jesus among us! It was an extraordinary experience.

We shall never, perhaps, be certain whether or not he is present in our midst at any given moment, for his presence presupposes the life of grace in us, and nobody can ever be quite sure if he is in a state of grace.

Yet there is no doubt that whenever our living together was based on a sincere readiness to die, if need be, for one another, after the example of Jesus, and when our whole lives were conformed to this basic attitude—for, " Above all things have a constant mutual charity "—then it often seemed to us that we experienced, with simplicity, his presence among us.

We might put it this way: just as a person feels joy or sorrow, anguish or doubt, so too—but in a higher part of the soul—we experienced the peace that only the spiritual presence of Jesus in our midst could give; the fullness of joy to be found only in him, the vigor and conviction which are less the fruit of reasoning or an effort of the will, than of a special help from God.

His presence was a more than sufficient recompense for any sacrifice that we made. It gave meaning and purpose to every step we took along our way, toward him and for his sake. It enabled us to see things and circumstances in their proper perspective, comforted us in our troubles, and tempered any excessive rejoicing.

Whoever among us, without over-rationalizing or complicating things, would believe in his words, with the simple fascination of a child, and put them into practice, could enjoy this foretaste of paradise, the kingdom of God in the midst of those who are united in his name.

Jesus in our midst! This is what our living together means.

And yet, it was when, through some fault of ours, he was no longer in our midst, that we better understood what this presence of Jesus had meant to us.

At such times we did not feel at all tempted to return to the world we had left behind. The experience of " Jesus in our midst " had been too real and profound for us to be any longer attracted by the vanities of this world. It was his divine presence that had made us see these vanities in their true proportions, as worthless.

Instead, like shipwrecked persons who cling to any spar that will keep them afloat, we sought for any means, suggested by the Gospel, to rebuild our shattered unity.

But it was not enough to make a firm act of the will when it seemed that he was no longer present among us. Logs of wood that are placed on the fire are consumed while they feed the flames. Similarly, to live with Jesus in our midst, we had to practice, moment by moment, all the virtues—patience, prudence, meekness, poverty, etc.—that enable us to maintain a constantly supernatural unity with each other. The presence of Jesus could not be procured once and for all, since it was a living, dynamic presence.

"Where two or three . . . . " We often had occasion to marvel at the effects produced by the practice of these divine and mysterious words.

"Where two or three . . . . " Jesus does not specify anybody in particular; the "two or three" are anonymous.

"Where two or three . . . " whoever they may be.

Two or three repentant sinners who unite in his name; two or three young women, as we were during the war; two, one of which is a grown-up, the other a child. Living these words we have seen barriers crumble on every side. Such has been the case with narrow, provincial mentalities, like the fault-finding prejudice and even hatred that one often sees in relations between people from different towns and regions. Jesus in the midst overcame these human miseries.

Where two or three of different nationalities are united, nationalistic prejudices vanish.

Where two or three of different races are united, racial feelings disappear.

Where two or three people belonging to cultural, social or age groups that have traditionally been at odds . . . .

All men can, indeed should, unite in the name of Christ.

Where two or three, even among the faithful

and the practicing Christians ... thus doing away with the closed-group mentality so often apparent in members of different religious associations and orders.

The practice of these words of the Gospel gave our gatherings and our community the flavor and atmosphere of the early Christian communities and helped show the world that the Church is a Mother to men of every kind, shining forth resplendently in her unity.

These words, furthermore, implied a communal Christian life, one that went beyond the purely individualistic, and now anachronistic, manner of life that many of us had previously led.

It was a spirituality which did not require any lengthy process of preparation, nor was it open exclusively to chosen souls or those already adept in spiritual things. It seemed an ideal made for all. Jesus, in fact, did not say: " Where two or three saints are gathered in my name ... " but, " Where two or three .... "

To know what the presence of Jesus means, one must experience it. One example, however, that is helpful in explaining it, is the Gospel story of the two disciples on their way to Emmaus.

Some years back we visited the Holy Land,

and this for us was a unique experience. It was a real grace of God to go from one Holy Place to another, receiving so many profound impressions. One of these places was Emmaus, where we went one afternoon. A golden sunset awaited us when we got there, and as we left the car and walked on the ground where perhaps Jesus had once trod, we recalled the events that had occurred there many years ago.

Two disciples, coming from Jerusalem, were heading for Emmaus, a small town about seven miles from Jerusalem. Jesus had been dead three days, and had then risen on the third.

As the two disciples walked along, they saw a man draw near and walk alongside them. " What is this conversation which you are holding with each other as you walk? " he asked them. " And they stood still, looking sad." One of them replied: " Are you the only visitor to Jerusalem who does not know the things that have happened there in these days . . . concerning Jesus of Nazareth, who was a prophet mighty in deed and word . . . and how our chief priests . . . crucified him? " " O foolish men, and slow of heart," answered Jesus. " Was it not necessary that the Christ should suffer these things . . . ? " And he went on to explain the Scriptures to them.

When they reached Emmaus, the disciples saw

that he made a gesture as if to leave them, and they invited him to stay with them: " Stay with us, for it is toward evening and the day is now far spent."

So he went in with them, and at the breaking of the bread, they recognized who he was. But he immediately disappeared from their sight.

And they said to one another: " Did not our hearts burn within us while he talked to us . . . ? "

There are probably no better words than these to explain the experience that we have had from the time we started living with Jesus in our midst. Jesus is always himself, and even when he is present only spiritually, he explains the Scriptures to us, and our hearts burn with the charity of Christ, which is the true life. Once we have known him this way, we are tempted to say, with infinite nostalgia: " ' Stay with us, for it is toward evening,' and without you it is indeed dark night."

In all these years the effects of his presence have been immense.

It is Jesus who touches men's hearts. He alone knows how to convert people; he alone can truly bear witness to himself. And as a result, around those who have left all things, both materially and spiritually, for the sake of the precious pearl of the Gospel, things tend to change.

Few remain indifferent when they come in contact with Jesus present in a small or large community. Jesus, who is the Light, manifests himself; he who is the Fire, gives out warmth. So that many who never really believed in him before, begin to believe, because now, in a way, spiritually, they have seen him.

Many non-believers, atheists, public sinners, drunks, women of the streets, have been totally transformed and have become followers of Christ.

Persons who were vacillating in their faith, or indifferent, priests who were tormented by difficulties in their vocation, on meeting Jesus in the midst of persons supernaturally united, have found new ardor and peace of soul, new meaning in the life they had embarked upon, additional strength in doing God's will.

And just as Jesus, when he was on earth, did not limit himself to saving the souls of men, so Jesus among us has shown us the way to get material favors also.

Living in the light of his presence, we were able to understand better, and apply on a wide scale, the words of our Lord: " If two of you agree on earth about anything they ask, it will be done for them by my Father in heaven."

So each time we had a particular spiritual or material favor to pray for, we did so together. And innumerable were the graces received, of every kind, that strongly suggested a supernatural intervention.

This has become the characteristic form of prayer in the Movement.

Another effect of His presence among us must be noted. Just as in the beginning it seemed that our deepened understanding of the Scriptures must have been due to the presence of Jesus among us, so too, we felt it must have been this same presence that enabled us to understand more profoundly the words of the Holy Father and the bishops.

Their teaching found an echo in our souls.

Dogmas, too, that we had sometimes heard criticized by teachers who were non-believers or of weak faith, now acquired the savor of truth, not because we were obliged to accept them blindly, but because they had somehow become less obscure to us and, while remaining in the area of mystery, were not devoid of a certain comprehensibility.

It was this *sense* of the Church, of the hierarchy and the Church's doctrine, that convinced us that such a life was capable of forming real champions of the Church, able to defend her against errors, not so much through the study of theology—which, however, if properly used, can be of great value in this area—as through this inward comprehension of the Church, this sharing in its nature that the soul experiences.

Such a spirituality could form persons able to cooperate in one of today's most pressing tasks: the dialogue with the world.

It is this *sense* of the truth that makes it possible for one to approach those who are in error, and to appreciate that minimum of truth that every man believes in, so as to throw a bridge between Christians and non-Christians, and prepare the ground for the further evangelization of men.

If we were asked what else Jesus in our midst means to us in the Movement, we would say that he has been its *founder* and *legislator*. The Movement is now beginning to possess a structure of its own, even juridically speaking, but this has proved possible only through the gradual application of the different ideas that it seems Jesus in the midst of us, united together and united to the hierarchy, has suggested day by day.

Jesus in our midst has also been the best *propagator* of the Movement, through the testimony of unity that has been given: " That they may all be one ... that the world may believe .... "

He is also the chief *mainstay* of the Movement. His presence has nearly always been our one and only comfort, even in the hardest and most difficult moments for the Movement, both at its center and in every part of the world where it exists.

If it is powerful in its effects, it is due to him, and if it has been officially recognized by the Church, this is because one and the same Christ lives in the Movement and in the Hierarchy of the Church.

He is our *leader* on all the fronts of the battle that we must wage, the fronts that are already established and only need to be maintained and expanded, and the new fronts that Jesus opens up to us from time to time, which we never previously imagined we would one day have to confront. God's plan for the Movement is in God himself, and in him only, and it is Jesus in our midst who gradually makes clear to us further aspects of it.

Jesus in our midst is also the real *superior* of every community of whatever size in the Movement. Through the charity that circulates among all, he enlightens those whose task it is to guide the others. But this he does also through the particular grace that superiors have to teach the others, first and foremost, always to give priority to having Jesus in the midst.

When a branch of the Movement, or a center or whole region of the Movement is constituted in the way God has shown us and the Church has confirmed, we may say that God speaks through the superiors; in this Movement, raised up, nourished, molded and formed by him, they have no other duty than to interpret his wishes.

When Jesus is among us, *wisdom,* with ceaseless activity, seems to order all things. Each one shares in it and takes joy in it, feeling, wherever he may be, that he occupies the right place, the place God wants for him.

From the smallest center to the families where this spirit is lived; from two politicians who unite together in the name of Jesus to a group of Benedictines who live this ideal to those who work for its diffusion in America or Africa . . . wherever there exists a cell, a nucleus of this Movement, there the light of Jesus in our midst shines forth brilliantly.

And the presence of Jesus makes us, in a way, similar to Mary, that is, instruments in giving Jesus, spiritually, to the world.

At the beginning we left all things in order to choose God alone. When we practice this spirituality God has given us, putting his will into effect, it seems that the supreme and unique ideal we chose when we were surrounded by the shatters of war, comes down and dwells among us: Jesus, in our midst.